COUNT
With Clifford
THE BIG RED DOG®

**Activities for Building
Fine-Motor and Early Math Skills**

SCHOLASTIC

New York • Toronto • London • Auckland • Sydney
Mexico City • New Delhi • Hong Kong • Buenos Aires

FREE Activity Book Online!
Go to teacherexpress.scholastic.com/Clifford

™ & © Scholastic Inc. SCHOLASTIC and associated logo is a trademark of Scholastic Inc.
CLIFFORD THE BIG RED DOG and associated logo is a trademark of Norman Bridwell. All rights reserved.

Originally published as *Little Kids . . . Count!*
Cover design by Michelle Kim
Written and illustrated by Karen Sevaly

ISBN: 978-0-545-81961-1
Copyright © 2015 by Scholastic Inc.
All rights reserved. Published by Scholastic Inc.
Printed in the U.S.A.

2 3 4 5 6 7 8 9 10   40   21 20 19 18 17 16 15

Contents

Welcome to the wonderful world of young learners, where learning is like play with everyone's much-loved canine—Clifford The Big Red Dog®! This book offers easy activities that will help your child develop the skills needed to meet key early curriculum standards and succeed in school. The activities provide practice in writing the numbers 1–20, counting to 20, matching numbers and sets, and more.

Each activity page targets specific skills for your child to practice. The consistent format will help your child work independently and with self-assurance. Other important features include:

- easy-to-follow directions to help build vocabulary, as well as early math and reading comprehension skills

- tracing, writing, drawing, coloring, and matching exercises to develop and strengthen your child's visual perception and discrimination, eye-hand coordination, and fine-motor skills

- appealing artwork that engages and motivates your child to learn

On the following pages, you'll find suggestions for introducing the activity pages to your child, tips for getting started and making the experience go smoothly, plus activities you can do with your child to extend learning.

We hope you and your child enjoy doing the activities in this book. Your involvement will help make this a valuable educational experience and will support and enhance your child's learning. And with Clifford The Big Red Dog® along for company, it's sure to be filled with fun!

What's Inside

Most young children naturally begin expressing mathematical concepts as they discover the world around them. As young learners progress in cognitive skills through play, they can learn to recognize and understand simple number concepts. The activities in this book have been designed for the developmental abilities of your young child. The large-size numbers and number words and the wide guide lines offer support as your child practices tracing. These features let your child experience success, helping build self-esteem and confidence. Page 5 provides a close-up look at the different kinds of activities in this book.

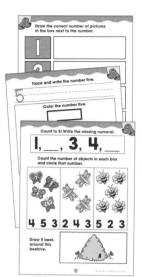

Trace and Write Numbers

(pages 7–40)

On these pages, your child traces, writes, and colors to practice and learn the numbers 1 to 20. Numbered directional arrows indicate the correct order in which to form each number. The "Count to . . ." pages include simple number lines and opportunities for your child to draw and color to practice counting up to 20. The "Draw the Number" pages invite your child to draw pictures to represent a given number.

Trace Number Words

(pages 41 and 42)

To build recognition of number words, your child practices tracing the words for the numbers 1 to 10.

Count and Paste Numbers

(pages 43 and 45)

Your child counts the number of objects in different groups, then cuts and pastes the correct number in the blank boxes.

Achievement Certificates

(page 47)

After your child has completed the activity pages, acknowledge his or her efforts by completing the "I Know Numbers!" and "I Can Count to 20!" certificates. Post them on the refrigerator or on a bulletin board to honor your child's achievements.

Helpful Tips

- For ease of use, simply choose the skills you would like your child to work on (you'll find detailed information on the Contents page), locate the corresponding activity page in the book, and gently tear out the page along the perforated edges.

- The only materials needed for the activities are crayons, child-safe scissors, and glue or glue sticks.

- Help your child read the directions on the activity pages.

- Let your child complete each activity page at his or her own pace.

- Review the completed pages together and encourage your child to share the thinking behind his or her responses.

- Support your child's efforts and offer help when needed.

- Display your child's work and share his or her progress with family and friends!

Extending Learning

Here are a few ideas to give your child more practice developing number sense and counting skills.

Number Sense

🐾 Use your finger to trace a number on your child's back and have him or her name the number. Then let your child trace a number on your back for you to guess.

🐾 Have your child place one hand on a sheet of construction paper and trace around it using a marker. Then have your child count the number of fingers on the tracing. Write the corresponding numbers (1 to 5) on the fingers of the tracing and encourage your child to use the pattern for number practice. (You can also trace both hands to practice 1 to 10.)

🐾 Ask your child to answer questions, such as *I'm thinking of a number that tells me how many buttons are on my shirt; I'm thinking of a number between 3 and 5; I'm thinking of a number that tells me how old you are.*

Counting

🐾 Have your child line up small objects, such as buttons, cotton balls, pennies, or paper clips, and count them.

🐾 Give your child a long shoelace that you've knotted at one end. Encourage your child to count out a given number of large beads and string them on the shoelace.

🐾 Place a large number of small objects in a paper bag. Have your child reach in with one hand and grab as many as possible. Help your child count out the number in his or her hand. Replace the items and repeat the activity.

🐾 At snack time, help your child spread cream cheese onto a cracker or celery stalk, then count out a given number of raisins to place on top.

🐾 Invite your child to practice counting around your home, for example, the number of windows in a room, spoons in a drawer, or toys as he or she puts them away.

Trace and write the number one.

Color the number one.

Count to 1!

Trace and write the number two.

Color the number two.

Count to 2!

Trace and write the number three.

3

Color the number three.

Count to 3!

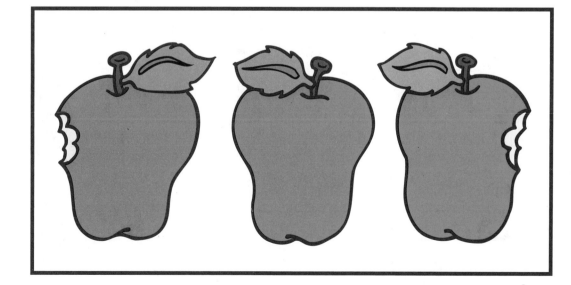

1 —————————— 2 —————————— 3

Color 3 pencils.

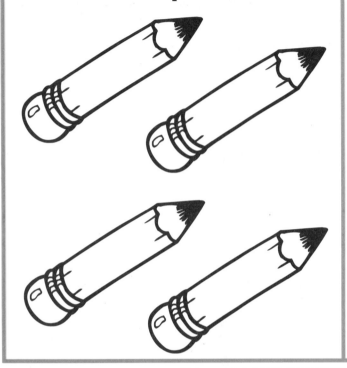

Color 3 scissors.

Draw a line to match the number to the correct number of objects.

2

1

3

Count to 3! Write the missing numeral.

1, 2, __

Count the number of objects in each box and circle that number.

3 1 2   **2 3 1**   **1 3 2**

Draw 3 spots on the dog.

Trace and write the number four.

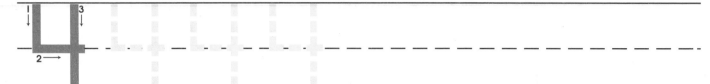

Color the number four.

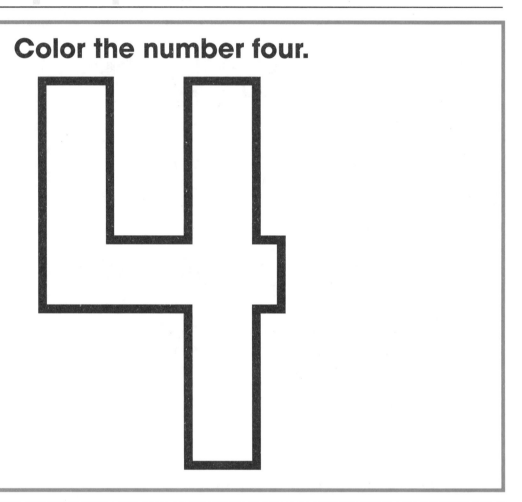

Count to 4!

Trace and write the number five.

5 5 5 5 5

Color the number five.

Count to 5!

Count to 5!

1   2   3   4   5

Color 5 butterflies.

Color 5 snails.

Draw a line to match the number to the correct number of objects.

4

5

3

Count to 5! Write the missing numeral.

1, ___, 3, 4, ___

Count the number of objects in each box and circle that number.

4 5 3   2 4 3   5 2 3

Draw 5 bees around this beehive.

Count With Clifford The Big Red Dog® © Scholastic Inc.

Draw the correct number of pictures in the box next to the number.

1	
2	
3	
4	
5	

Trace and write the number six.

6

Color the number six.

Count to 6!

Trace and write the number seven.

7

Color the number seven.

Count to 7!

Trace and write the number eight.

Color the number eight.

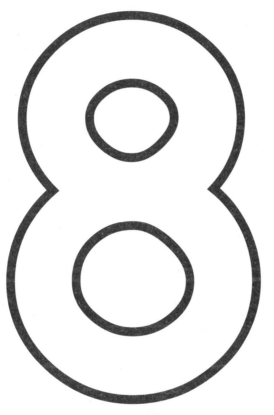

Count to 8!

Trace and write the number nine.

Color the number nine.

Count to 9!

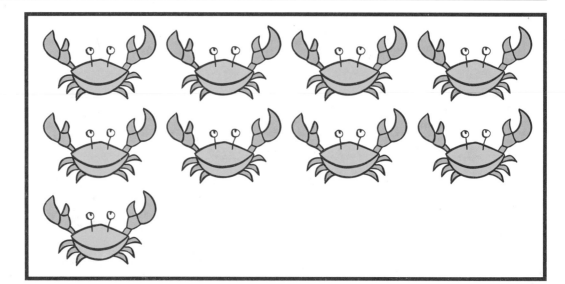

Trace and write the number ten.

Color the number ten.

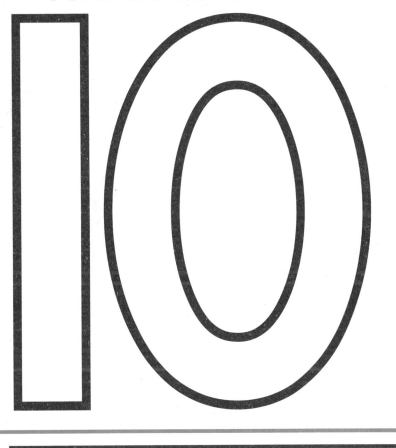

Count to 10!

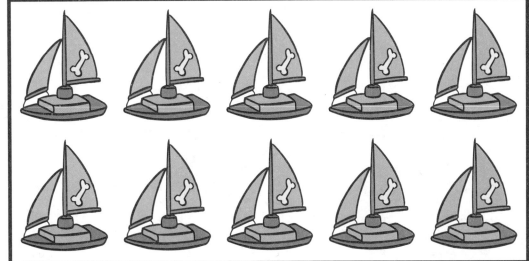

Count to 10!

1 2 3 4 5 6 7 8 9 10

Color 10 fish.   Color 10 turtles.

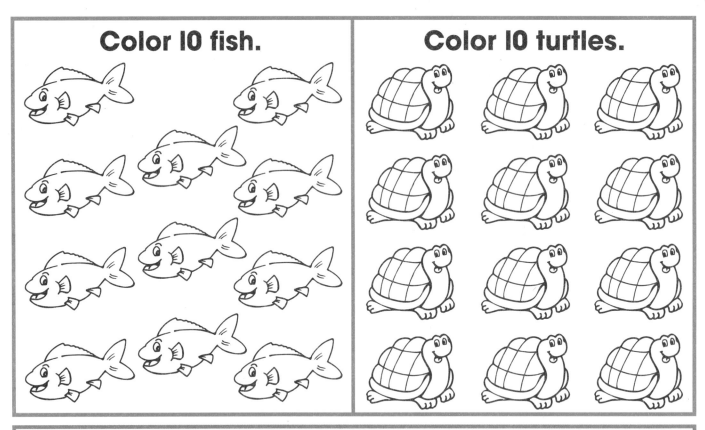

Draw a line to match the number to the correct number of objects.

10   8   9

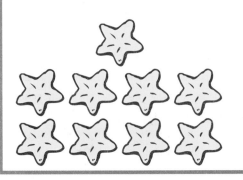
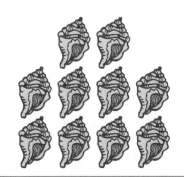
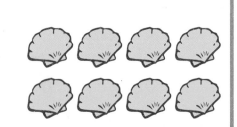

Count to 10! Write the missing numeral.

1, 2, __, 4, 5, __, 7, 8, __, 10

Count the number of objects in each box and circle that number.

8 6 9   **10 6 7**   **9 7 10**

Draw 10 fish in the fishbowl.

Draw the correct number of pictures in the box next to the number.

6	
7	
8	
9	
10	

Trace and write the number eleven.

Color the number eleven.

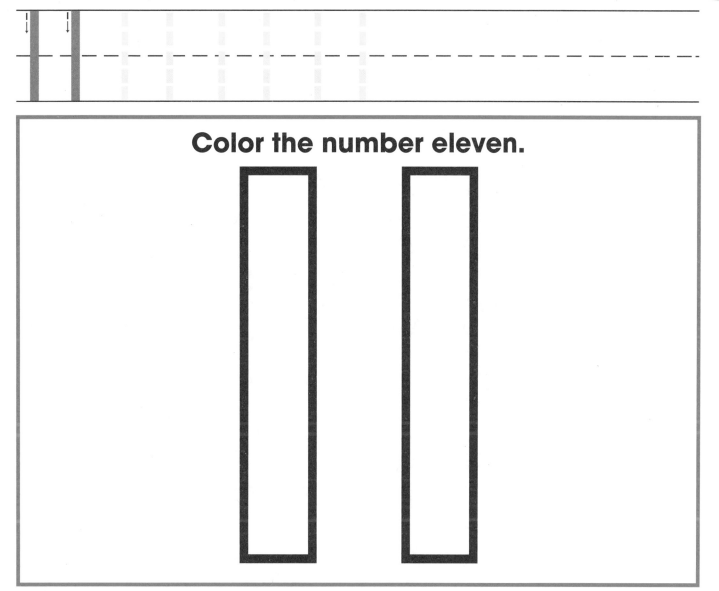

Count to 11!

Trace and write the number twelve.

Color the number twelve.

Count to 12!

Count With Clifford The Big Red Dog® © Scholastic Inc.

Trace and write the number thirteen.

Color the number thirteen.

Count to 13!

Trace and write the number fourteen.

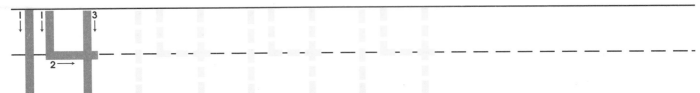

Color the number fourteen.

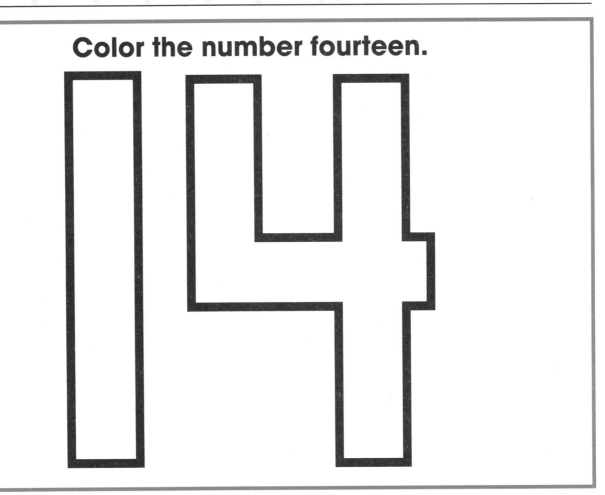

Count to 14!

Trace and write the number fifteen.

Color the number fifteen.

Count to 15!

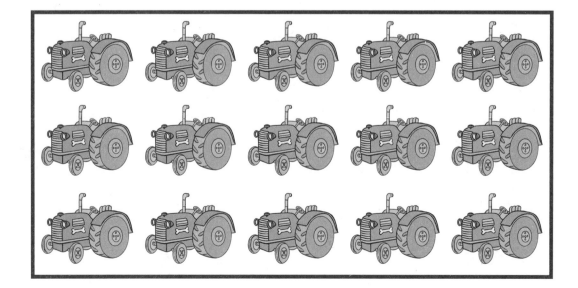

Count to 15!

1 2 3 4 5 6 7 8 9 10 11 12 13 14 15

Color 15 chickens.

Draw a line to match the number to the correct number of objects.

12   15   13

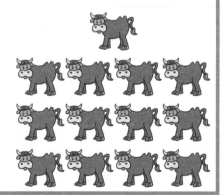

Count to 15! Write the missing numeral.

9, __, 11, 12, __, 14, __

Count the number of objects in each box and circle that number.

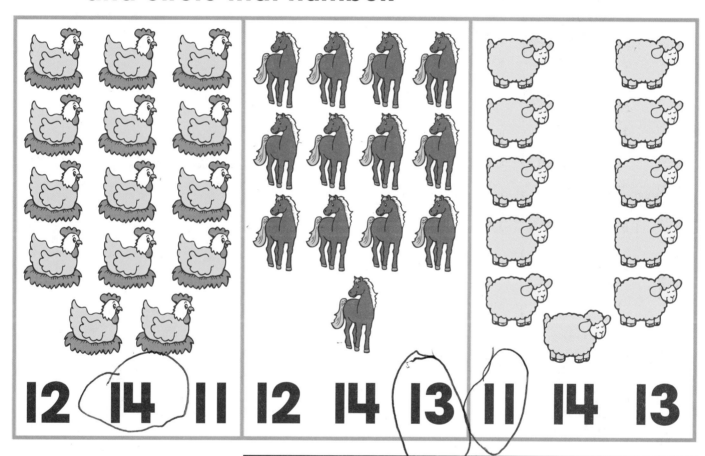

| 12 | (14) | 11 | 12 | 14 | (13) | (11) | 14 | 13 |

Draw 15 apples on the apple tree.

Draw the correct number of pictures in the box next to the number.

11	
12	
13	
14	
15	

Trace and write the number sixteen.

Color the number sixteen.

Count to 16!

Trace and write the number seventeen.

Color the number seventeen.

Count to 17!

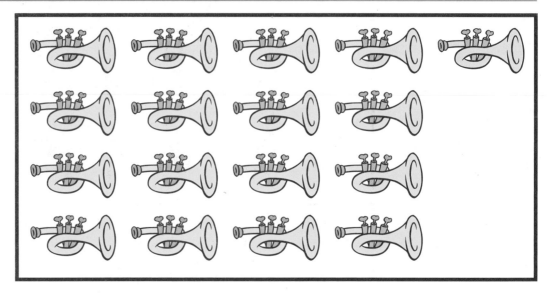

Trace and write the number eighteen.

Color the number eighteen.

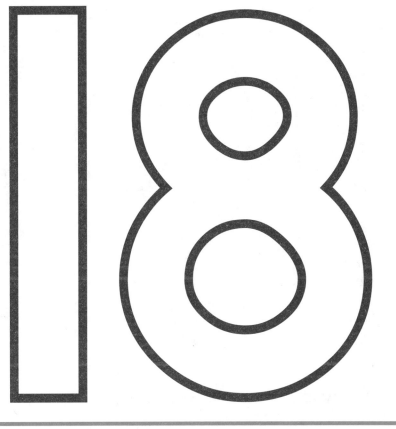

Count to 18!

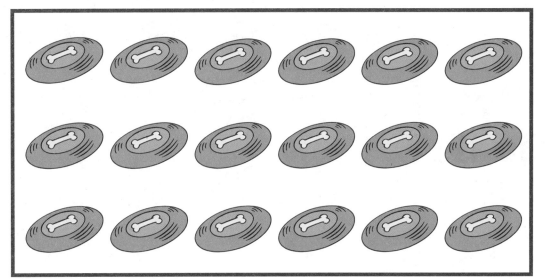

Trace and write the number nineteen.

Color the number nineteen.

Count to 19!

Count With Clifford The Big Red Dog® © Scholastic Inc.

Trace and write the number twenty.

20 20 20 20

Color the number twenty.

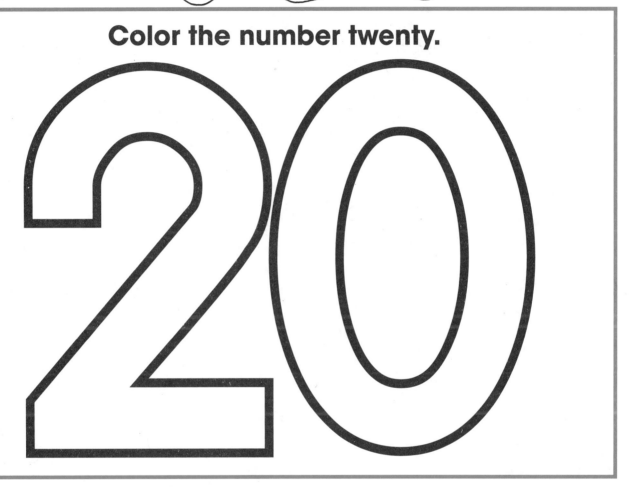

Count to 20!

Count to 20!

1	2	3	4	5	6	7	8	9	10	11	12	13	14	15	16	17	18	19	20

Color 20 bunnies.

Draw a line to match the number to the correct number of objects.

20   17   19

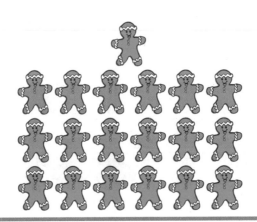

38

Count to 20! Write the missing numeral.

15, 16, ___, ___, 19, ___

Count the number of objects in each box and circle that number.

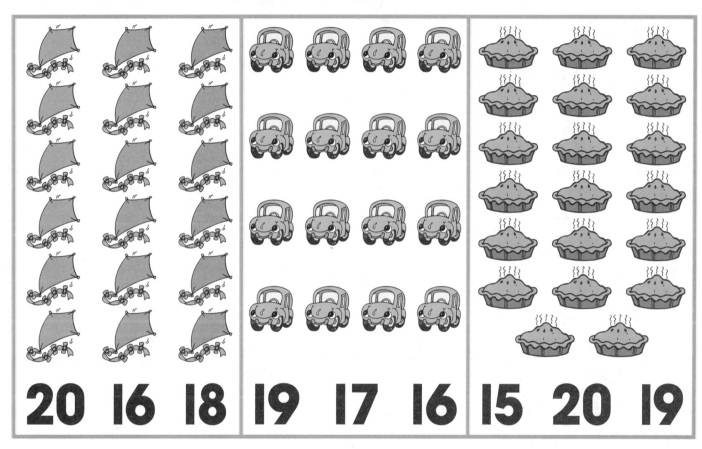

| 20 16 18 | 19 17 16 | 15 20 19 |

Draw 20 stars!

Draw the correct number of pictures in the box next to the number.

16	
17	
18	
19	
20	

Trace these number words.

1 one

2 two

3 three

4 four

5 five

Trace these number words.

6 ~~six~~

7 ~~seven~~

8 ~~eight~~

9 ~~nine~~

10 ~~ten~~

Count and Paste 1 to 6 Cut out the numbers at the bottom of the page. Count each group of objects and paste the correct number in the box.

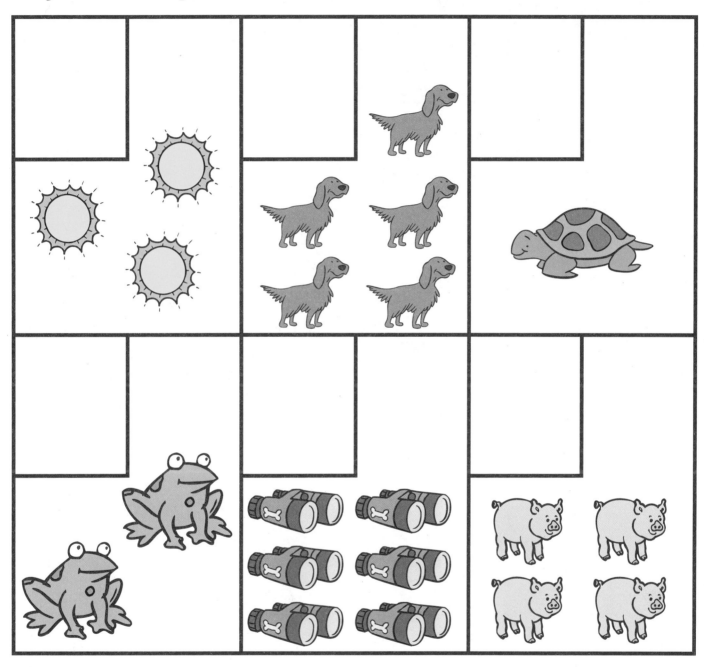

Count and Paste 7 to 12 Cut out the numbers at the bottom of the page. Count each group of objects and paste the correct number in the box.

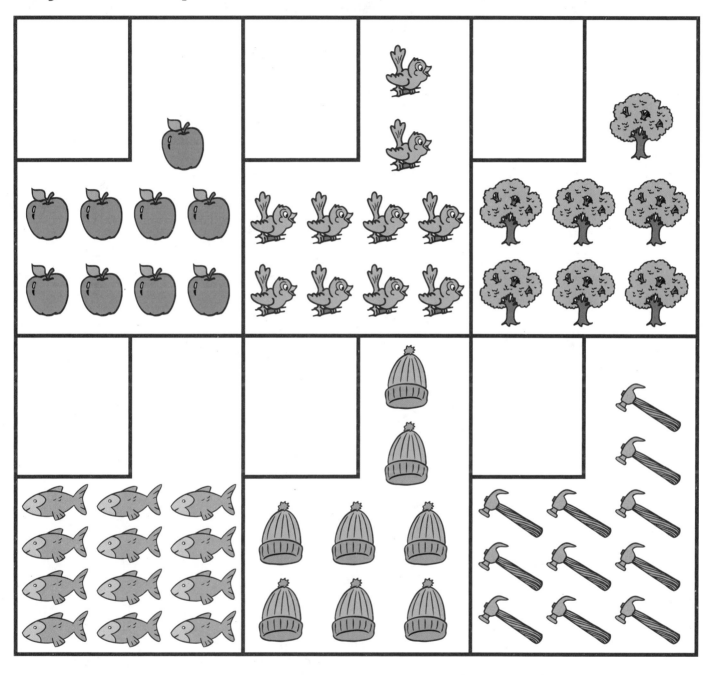

3 4
8
9 12
5

I Know Numbers!

_____
Name

_____
Parent

_____
Date

---

2 10
17
13
18
6

I Can Count to 20!

_____
Name

_____
Parent

_____
Date